Guided Journal *for* Women *with* Anxiety

Guided Journal *for* Women *with* Anxiety

Prompts and Practices to Release Worry,
Manage Stress, and Embrace Calm

AMANDA LANDRY, LMHC

ROCKRIDGE
PRESS

For general information on our other products and services or to obtain technical support, please contact our Customer Care Department within the United States at (866) 744-2665, or outside the United States at (510) 253-0500.

Rockridge Press publishes its books in a variety of electronic and print formats. Some content that appears in print may not be available in electronic books, and vice versa.

Interior and Cover Designer: John Calmeyer
Art Producer: Hannah Dickerson
Editor: Chloe Moffett
Production Manager: Sandy Norman and Lanore Coloprisco
Production Editor: Melissa Edeburn

Author photo courtesy of Blue Anchor Love Photography

Paperback ISBN: 978-1-63807-361-1
R0

This journal belongs to:

Contents

Introduction

T hank you for choosing to start your journey to manage your anxiety with this book. You are here because you want to get control of your anxiety and learn specific strategies to help you manage it. You probably have struggled with anxiety much of your life. You may have tried other ways to manage it, but you're ready to try this journal.

Anxiety is an emotion characterized by feelings of tension, worried thoughts, and physical changes in the body. Physical symptoms related to anxiety include sweating, trembling, dizziness, and a rapid heartbeat. People with anxiety can also experience intrusive thoughts, worries, and concerns. A lot of people will avoid people, places, and things that contribute to their anxiety.

Many women struggle with anxiety. Life can be very stressful with all the demands placed on women. It's not uncommon to get overwhelmed, and many women express overwhelm as anxiety. You are not alone in your struggles with anxiety. The National Institute of Mental Health reported that 23.4 percent of women expressed feeling anxiety within the past year. That number represents almost one in four women. Again, you are not alone in your struggle with anxiety, and this book was written with you in mind.

I come from a family of anxious women. Growing up, I was taught that bad things can and will happen. My belief system became "I must prepare for the bad things that will happen." This teaching led to an over-developed sense of responsibility for others as well as myself. I felt like I had to take care of myself and others so that the "bad things" wouldn't happen. I would feel anxious thinking about terrible things that could happen, and then I would feel anxious when making my contingency plans for the catastrophes. By the time I was in my 20s, my anxiety was no longer manageable, and I started therapy with a wonderful woman who helped me put my life back together. This belief system is part of what drew me to being a therapist. Through therapy, journaling, reading, and personal development work, I've learned to challenge the belief systems that tell me, "Bad things happen, you can stop them from happening, and you need to make sure they don't happen to other people."

When anxiety is no longer manageable or affects your daily life, it may be an anxiety disorder. Common anxiety disorders include generalized anxiety disorder, post-traumatic stress disorder, panic disorder, and phobias. It is important to speak with a mental health professional if you suspect you have an anxiety disorder. This journal can be used in conjunction with therapy to help you achieve your mental health goals.

Journaling for anxiety is a common and popular way to manage the symptoms of anxiety. Research shows that expressing your feelings and putting them down on paper helps strengthen your mental health and the ability to cope with stressors. Positive affirmations are an easy and fun way to incorporate healthy belief systems. Practicing healthy coping skills is a foundational tool in managing anxiety. One of the first things I ask my patients to do is to create a list of healthy coping skills to use. This book outlines tools you can start using today.

Being a therapist has taught me that people can learn to control their anxiety. This book is intended to share the strategies I've learned over the years to control anxiety. The tools in this journal are based on evidence-based treatments, such as cognitive behavioral therapy (CBT), dialectical behavioral therapy (DBT), and attachment-focused therapy. CBT is a therapeutic intervention that focuses on challenging and changing cognitive distortions and behaviors, thus reducing symptoms of anxiety. DBT uses strategies to help people live in the moment, cope with stressors, regulate their emotions, and increase interpersonal skills. Attachment-focused therapy works on building trust in relationships and learning how to express emotions.

You can and will get control of your anxiety. This is the start of your wellness journey. Your healing begins now.

How to Use This Journal

By using this journal, it is my intention for you to explore the underlying belief systems that create anxiety for you. Once you know the belief systems that contribute to your anxiety, you can begin to challenge them and use other tools to help manage your symptoms.

This journal is intended to guide you down a path of wellness to help you manage your anxiety. The prompts are meant for you to dig deep and explore your anxiety and the factors that contribute to it. The practices are exercises you can do on a regular basis to help regulate your mind, body, and soul. The positive affirmations are reminders of all the goodness inside of you.

One of my favorite activities for positive affirmations is to put them all around the house, on your phone, and anywhere you spend a lot of time. When you see your positive affirmations regularly, their messaging will begin to shift from your conscious mind to your subconscious mind.

By completing the prompts, you will begin to explore your internal experience around your anxiety. During the exploration process, you will look at your past, present, and future and learn how your anxiety was developed, the relationships that contribute to it, how to manage it, and what you want your life to look like with your anxiety under control.

Take your time to reflect on the prompts. The longer prompts may take up to 20 minutes for you to think about, write your thoughts, and process any emotions that come up. The short prompts are designed for you to write your response within five minutes. After completing a prompt, spend time experiencing any feelings that came up, and, if needed, write down how you are feeling at the end of the prompt. These prompts can be completed every day to help keep you accountable for working through your anxiety.

The exercises are guideposts for you to use to improve overall wellness in your life. Try each of them, and pick your favorites to practice whenever you are feeling anxious.

This book was written to be easy and engaging for you. Enjoy the process and remember that you have got this!

I define myself through the strength, calm, and happiness in my life. My anxiety does not get to define me.

Discuss the first time you remember being anxious. How old were you, and what was going on that made you anxious? How did you handle your anxiety? How did other people around you respond to your anxiety? What did you learn about anxiety then?

_____

_____

_____

_____

_____

_____

_____

_____

_____

_____

_____

_____

_____

_____

_____

_____

_____

List 10 symptoms of your anxiety and how they impact you, such as being worried, expecting the worst to happen, or feeling tension in your chest. How do these symptoms show up in your life on a regular basis? How can you learn to manage them? Write down one or two ways you can manage each symptom, such as stopping your thoughts or doing breath work.

S hare a time when you were able to handle your anxiety in a healthy way. What did you do that impacted you positively? How did that situation turn out for you? How can you handle your anxiety in the future?

_____

_____

_____

_____

_____

_____

_____

_____

_____

_____

_____

_____

_____

_____

_____

_____

_____

_____

Dancing is an easy and fun way to get in touch with your body and burn off some excess energy. One of the first things you'll want to do to manage anxiety is to increase pleasurable activities, and dancing can go at the top of that list. Don't worry if you aren't a "good" dancer. You can just sway to the music and be present in the moment. All you have to do is put on some music and move your hips, feet, arms, or whatever feels good to you. Dancing in crowds can be a lot of fun, too. That is why dancing is so popular at weddings and birthday parties. If you are self-conscious or the thought of dancing makes you feel more anxious, dance in any way that feels safe and good to you. Put on some music while getting ready in the morning and shake your groove thing.

I am healthy, happy, and living the life of my dreams. Each day, my dreams are realized through my actions.

elf-soothing helps calm your nervous system and brings about relaxation in your body. List 10 ways you can self-soothe to manage anxiety, such as hugging a comfort blanket, drinking a hot cup of tea, or stretching parts of your body that feel tense. How have you used self-soothing in the past? What strategies can you use in the future to soothe anxiety?

_____

_____

_____

_____

_____

_____

_____

_____

_____

_____

_____

_____

_____

_____

_____

_____

_____

_____

_____

Forgiveness involves letting go of the burden that holding on to an event brings you. It does not involve forgiving those who have hurt you and allowing them to hurt you again. Forgiveness is coming to peace with what happened to you and letting go of the story that you are a victim. It's about taking back control of your life and letting go of something that no longer serves you. Write letters of forgiveness to those who have hurt you. Let them know you are letting go of the pain they have caused you. You can use the space provided on the next page or use a separate journal, stationery, or whatever is meaningful to you. Let them know you are not inviting them back into your life to hurt you again, but rather you are releasing any negative energy associated with the event. Burn a candle every day, and when you light it, speak out the names of the people you are forgiving as a symbol of detachment.

Gratitude is a great way to remind yourself of the good in your life and the context of your day-to-day experiences. Name five things you are grateful for, such as your family, friends, career, or even small things, like a hot cup of coffee in the morning. How does gratitude show up in your life? How can you practice gratitude every day for the small things?

_____

_____

_____

_____

_____

_____

_____

_____

_____

_____

_____

_____

_____

_____

_____

_____

Yoga is a healthy coping skill you can use to manage your anxiety. There are a lot of videos on YouTube that are designed to incorporate anxiety reduction through yoga. Yoga incorporates breath work with stretching and movement. Those combinations help bring calmness to your nervous system. Regular practice of yoga will help calm your sympathetic and parasympathetic nervous systems by teaching your body to relax and stop interpreting certain events as dangerous. Yoga will also teach you mindfulness skills that can help you stay present in the moment. The practice of yoga will elicit an overall feeling of relaxation and well-being, thus reducing anxiety. Yoga also helps you be present with yourself and learn not to compare yourself to other people. This is an important concept for managing anxiety because this is your journey, and you cannot compare it to anyone else's.

How do you want to feel in the morning when you wake up? Describe what a perfect day would look like for you. Where would you be, and what would you be doing? How would this perfect day differ from most days for you?

Write a letter to your body. Describe how you feel toward your body. Ask your body for what you need, especially related to your stress levels, anxiety, and feelings of overwhelm. Invite your body to bring calm, peace, relaxation, and strength to your narrative.

Being in nature can rejuvenate your mental health. When exploring the outdoors, make it a whole sensory experience. Use all five of your senses to note the sights, sounds, smells, feels, and tastes of nature. Taste fresh-picked berries on a summer day. Feel the texture of leaves and the warmth of the sun on your skin. Smell the fresh dew early in the morning. Listen for small animals making noises or the rustling of leaves. Look at the sights before you and take them all in. Create an experience for yourself and soak up all that nature has to offer to you to help keep you present in the moment. We call this *nature therapy*. Being in nature reduces stress and anxiety by teaching you to use your five senses to get in touch with the moment. How can you use this form of mindfulness to help manage your anxiety?

I am a strong, resilient, and stress-free woman. Stress no longer serves me in my life, and I let stress go.

O ur values inform our belief systems and our goals in life. List 10 of your values and how they are represented in your life. Values include things such as honesty, trust, balance, fun, happiness, knowledge, kindness, peace, responsibility, and wealth. Share about how each value impacts your mental health and the decisions you make about how to manage your anxiety.

---

common trigger of anxiety is a lack of boundaries or people crossing over your boundaries. It's important to have firm but flexible boundaries in your life. Boundaries mean saying no when you don't want to do something. They mean knowing what kind of behaviors you are willing and unwilling to tolerate in your life. Having boundaries means you are willing to leave situations when your boundaries have been ignored or crossed. When people don't set boundaries, they often feel overwhelmed with the commitments they make or the way other people treat them. Where can you begin to set boundaries in your life? How would your life look different if you started to say no? Practice saying no in three situations where you would normally struggle with setting boundaries.

Make a list of things within your control and another list of things that are not within your control. For example, you don't have control over how other people behave, but you do have control over how you respond. How do the things within your control contribute to your anxiety? How do the things outside it contribute to your anxiety? What can you do to let go of the things outside of your control?

_____

_____

_____

_____

_____

_____

_____

_____

_____

_____

_____

_____

_____

_____

_____

_____

eflecting on the positive can help turn around an anxious day. List five good things that have happened to you lately. Maybe you got a promotion at work or a friend sent you a nice gift. Write about each experience and how it has shaped your life. What happened in each of those experiences that brought you joy and happiness?

_____

_____

_____

_____

_____

_____

_____

_____

_____

_____

_____

_____

_____

_____

_____

_____

_____

_____

Ten minutes a day of meditation is all you need. You've probably heard from a few sources the benefits of meditation practice, which can include a sense of calm and peacefulness as well as an open-hearted willingness to manage all of life's day-to-day fluctuations. Find a quiet place for you to practice meditation. Sit up straight, close your eyes, and begin to meditate. You can do this solo, or you can use guided meditations, where someone guides you with words that will bring you to greater relaxation. YouTube has a plethora of guided meditations, especially ones for reducing stress, anxiety, worry, and fear. Whether you prefer guided or unguided meditation, the key to benefiting from meditation is maintaining a regular practice. Set aside time each day for reflection and quiet. Once you can control and reduce the chatter in your mind, you'll experience more calmness and peace in your life. Meditation is meant to help you challenge the unhealthy belief systems and uncontrollable thoughts that lead to anxiety by focusing on the here and now and not wandering off into worries or concerns.

elf-care is a must for managing your mental health. What are you doing to take time for yourself, such as exercising, eating a healthy meal, treating yourself to a massage, or taking a long, hot bath? How are you showing up each day to take care of yourself? How do you feel when you take time for yourself? How can you incorporate self-care every day?

Managing triggers is a proactive way to deal with anxiety. What are some of the triggers of your anxiety, and how do you manage them? Name three ways you can manage each trigger, such as with self-soothing skills, thought-changing exercises, or other healthy coping skills you enjoy. How can you work on reducing some of the triggers in your life?

I love myself through my journey with anxiety. Love and light enter my body, and anxious feelings leave my body.

Having a good support system is one of the most important tools for reducing anxiety and maintaining your emotional well-being. Having people you can trust is a must, because we all need someone to lean on in our times of need. Schedule regular times to meet with friends, and focus on the connection. Set up times to engage in healthy self-disclosure with one another, like talking about the anxiety and stress in your life. Make it a mini group therapy session among your closest confidants. Talk about what's going on in your life, ask for support, and provide support to those in your circle of friends. What impact do your friendships have on your mental health? Friendships have been proven to improve mental health, so be sure to foster relationships that support you on your journey. How can you use your support system in your times of need?

Eating healthy and nutritious food is one way to nourish your body and reduce anxiety. Look for foods that make your body and soul feel good. Your body will tell you what foods it likes and what foods don't work for you. Food is one way to connect and listen to your body. Eating healthy doesn't have to be restrictive, either; you're encouraged to celebrate with food. Using healthy foods to manage your anxiety does not mean that you can't enjoy cookies or chips. You should find foods that support your overall health and wellness journey and incorporate them on a regular basis to improve the mind-body connection. Try increasing fruits, vegetables, healthy fats, and whole grains in your diet. How can you pick foods that make your body feel good? What are some steps you can take to make peace with food?

Most of the time, anxiety manifests as worrying about the future. Sometimes our past anxieties can give us answers to our present-day worries. Think about something that made you anxious in the past. What can you learn about those circumstances that apply to your life today?

Anxiety often comes from thinking a lot about the future. Write a letter to your future self and focus on how you might feel with less anxiety. Describe how anxiety has affected your life and why it's important to minimize it moving forward.

_____

_____

_____

_____

_____

_____

_____

_____

_____

_____

_____

_____

_____

_____

_____

_____

_____

_____

Worry is a symptom of anxiety that can be managed by learning to identify your worries and then identifying strategies to control, stop, and release them. Write down everything you are worried about. Purge your worries below and get them out of your head. Just let yourself write until you stop, and don't censor yourself. Unburden yourself.

Breath work is one of the best things you can practice to reduce your anxiety. This tool can help you in the moment, as well as teach your nervous system to calm down in a variety of situations. Breathing is often the first line of defense for anxiety. By practicing breath work, you'll learn how to slow down your nervous system, thus reducing your body's reaction to stress and anxiety. A popular technique to help control breathing is to practice *square* or *box breathing*. You'll want to breathe in and out of your nose through a count of four. Breathe in for four, hold for four, breathe out for four, and hold for four. Try that flow for 10 cycles and notice how you feel after you're done. Make a commitment to increase deep breathing when you feel anxious and even when you feel calm. Deep and purposeful breathing signals to your body that it is okay to relax and is powerful when practiced regularly.

I am at peace with my body,
and my body is at peace with me.
Loving energy enters my body
to help release anxiety.

We all have an inner critic that tries to keep us on track in life, but their approach can be harsh. Write a letter to your inner critic. Thank them for keeping you accountable, but let them know you need a softer approach.

_____

_____

_____

_____

_____

_____

_____

_____

_____

_____

_____

_____

_____

_____

_____

_____

_____

_____

Use entertainment to keep you calm. Everyone has different forms of entertainment that they like to use, like watching a favorite movie, listening to music, playing a board game with family or friends, completing a puzzle, going to sporting events, watching a comedy show, or really anything that they consider to be fun and light-hearted. Being entertained can bring you relief from anxiety because you will be focused on the fun you are having. Having fun, especially with others, can help you feel alive and connected. Find an activity that really brings you laughter and enjoyment. Incorporate entertainment into all aspects of your life. Listen to your favorite music on the way to work. Plan one fun activity per weekend to keep you from feeling over-whelmed. How can entertainment help keep you from feeling anxious?

Happiness is an antidote for anxiety, worry, and stress. Write about three times when you were happy. Describe how you were feeling, what you were doing, and who was with you. Share what made those times joyful.

Incorporate self-soothing activities into your stress management tool kit. They reduce anxiety and increase calmness. What are some self-soothing activities you can use in order to manage anxiety? You'll want to think about incorporating your five senses while you use a strategy. For example, if you take a hot shower to self-soothe, think about how the water feels on your body, how your body smells, how the water tastes, how the water looks coming down, and how the shower sounds as the water cascades over you. We often think of self-soothing as something we teach babies, but it is for adults, too. How can you use self-soothing tools to help you relax? The goal of self-soothing is to help regulate your emotional state and increase your ability to cope with stressors.

G iving back and investing in others can bring joy into your life. Write about a time when you made a difference in someone's life. What did you do for them? How did it impact them? How did it impact your mental health? Brainstorm ways you can make giving back a regular part of your life.

_____

_____

_____

_____

_____

_____

_____

_____

_____

_____

_____

_____

_____

_____

_____

_____

_____

_____

Describe your perfect day. What would it look like? Who would you be with during this day of bliss? Use your five senses to describe how it looks and feels. Tell your anxiety that it has no place when you are living your best life.

_____

_____

_____

_____

_____

_____

_____

_____

_____

_____

_____

_____

_____

_____

_____

_____

_____

I have something special to offer the world. I offer my gifts to the world by showing up every day for myself.

ick one word that resonates with you and write about it. For instance, choose a word like *strength*, *courage*, or *resilience* and write about how this word can remind you to increase calm and serenity in your life.

One part of yourself is your inner child, the innocent part of you from childhood, who lives in you regardless of your age. Connecting with your inner child is a way to learn about the roots of your anxiety and how it developed. As children, we are taught both good and bad things about ourselves, we internalize those messages, and our inner child is created. We carry those messages throughout our life, and our inner child can create anxiety when we allow them to make decisions from the wounded part of ourselves. Take some time to explore the messages you received as a child and think about how they show up in your life. Then you'll want to reconnect with that wounded part of you and reparent it with loving-kindness. By connecting with your inner child, you'll have the opportunity to bring out the fun and healthy side of you while soothing the wounded side that can cause anxiety. How can connecting with your inner child help you lower anxiety?

Write a letter to your inner child. Use your nondominant hand to write the letter. Tell your inner child how special they are to you.

_____

_____

_____

_____

_____

_____

_____

_____

_____

_____

_____

_____

_____

_____

_____

_____

_____

S hare a particularly memorable story from your childhood that impacted you. How did this story contribute to your anxiety? What did you learn about yourself from this memory? How did anxiety show up in your life as a child?

Progressive muscle relaxation is a technique in which you tense and relax various muscles to help bring optimal relaxation to your body. Usually, you'll start at the top of your body and move your way through all the major muscle groups until you get to your legs and feet. You'll want to find a script that resonates with you. (Look in the Resources section on page 146 to find an example of a script.) You can either record yourself saying the script or find a video on YouTube that guides you through the process. You can use this technique to help you sleep; try doing a sequence right before you go to bed. The release of tension in your body can help you fall asleep faster and sleep deeper and longer. Identify a few other times you might use this technique. How do you feel after practicing progressive muscle relaxation?

I treat myself with loving-kindness every day, and every day it gets easier to shower myself with love, serenity, calm, and happiness.

Identify your negative coping strategies and explore how you have used them in the past. Examples of negative coping skills include watching too much TV, eating mindlessly, or criticizing yourself. Make a list of them and write about how they have hurt you. Write a goodbye letter to those negative coping skills to let go of them.

Another strategy to manage anxiety, especially when there are underlying factors that contribute to your emotions, is trauma work. Big traumas and small traumas may be impacting you and creating anxiety. Big traumas may include natural disasters, violent crimes, school shootings, or abuse. Small traumas vary from person to person and may include a breakup, moving, losing a job, or the loss of a friendship. Find a therapist or a trauma-informed space where you can explore and heal your trauma. Two popular treatments for trauma include eye movement desensitization and reprocessing (EMDR) and trauma-informed cognitive behavioral therapy (CBT). You'll want to find a safe space to explore your trauma, so be sure to look for trauma-informed therapists, groups, and healing spaces. The goal of trauma work is to help you identify healthy coping skills to manage your trauma and anxiety. Use this space to consider possible traumas and how they might affect your anxiety. Is there anything that you try to avoid thinking about?

Make a list of five goals you have for your life. Make the list SMART: specific, measurable, attainable, realistic, and time-bound. For example: "I will journal for 10 minutes a day three days a week starting tomorrow for the next two months." Write about how you can celebrate once you achieve your goals. Be sure to include at least one goal regarding your anxiety.

Fear is a driving factor of anxiety. List 10 things you are afraid of, such as abandonment, spiders, escalators, or something bad happening. How is your fear triggered in your daily life? How does this impact your anxiety? What strategies can you use to overcome your fears?

_____

_____

_____

_____

_____

_____

_____

_____

_____

_____

_____

_____

_____

_____

_____

_____

_____

_____

_____

I am letting go of anything that does not serve me, including anxious feelings, worry, negative thoughts, and tense feelings in my body.

eel the fear and do it anyway," I like to say. Identify what you fear and work through it, even though the activity scares the daylights out of you. Anxiety makes us want to run, hide, and withdraw from life. Face your fears and do what you want to do. Take back the reins in your life, and don't allow anxiety to stop you. Where would you be able to "feel the fear and do it anyway" in your life? Recognize that you may feel anxious in a variety of situations, but that does not mean something bad is going to happen or that you are not supposed to act. Feel the fear and do it anyway, which is the definition of *courage*.

rite down a quote from anyone who inspires you below. What does the quote mean to you? How can you use this quote to help you on a tough day? How does this quote relate to anxiety?

_____

_____

_____

_____

_____

_____

_____

_____

_____

_____

_____

_____

_____

_____

_____

_____

_____

B e picky about the media you consume. You'll want to create parameters for media, such as setting a time limit per day and identifying which types of content are off-limits. Not all media is bad, and there are feel-good stories out there, but if you are watching or reading the news regularly and it's making you feel anxious, you'll want to limit what you consume. This is not about putting your head in the sand about what's going on in the world; it's about being purposeful and mindful about what you consume. How can you be picky about the media you consume? What type of media helps keep you calm and connected? Know your media limits and boundaries and exercise them when you start to feel overwhelmed.

Your teenage years are a formative time. Write a letter to your teenage self and give them the guidance and words you wish you had gotten at that age, such as "You will be successful in the future, just give yourself some time to grow up" or "Your friendships will work themselves out." What do you wish you had heard as a teen? What perspectives do you have now that would have been helpful to your younger self?

Share five things you wish other people knew about you and your anxiety, such as how it changes over time or shows up in different parts of your life. If they knew these things, what would change in your life? How would your life improve? How do those five things impact your relationships with others?

_____

_____

_____

_____

_____

_____

_____

_____

_____

_____

_____

_____

_____

_____

_____

_____

_____

_____

Describe what self-care means to you. How have you incorporated self-care into your life? What would you like to be doing more of in terms of self-care? What would happen to your anxiety if you increased self-care?

I embrace who I am at my core,
and I love all those parts of me.
I love myself truly and completely.

I dentifying your cognitive distortions, or harmful thought patterns, will help you gain better control over your thoughts, especially the ones causing you anxiety. Read through these descriptions of common distortions and note if any ring true for your experience.

* All-or-nothing thinking, or black-and-white thinking, makes it hard to see the nuance in situations.
* Overgeneralization is looking at one bad situation and assuming that pattern will always repeat.
* A mental filter, or disqualifying the positive, is when you focus on a single negative event and exclude anything positive.
* Mind reading, one form of jumping to conclusions, is assuming what another person is thinking.

Do any of these patterns sound familiar? When you feel anxious, write down any thoughts that you have. Reference this list, and work on identifying which distortion you might be using. Then try to create a new alternative positive thought and repeat it to yourself whenever you notice distorted thinking cropping up.

Read through these other common cognitive distortions and note any that might apply to you.

* Fortune telling (the other type of jumping to conclusions) is when you assume what will happen and make predictions without evidence.
* Magnification (catastrophizing) and minimization are defense mechanisms people use to manage their emotions by making a stressful situation seem more or less important than it really is.
* Emotional reasoning is when you accept your feelings as facts instead of examining them and thinking critically about situations.
* "Should" statements are demands that you make to yourself about what you "should," "ought to," or "must" do.
* Personalization is taking things personally or assigning blame to yourself when there is no logical reason you are at fault.

If any of these patterns strikes a nerve, write about it. Reference this list frequently, and begin to become aware of your distortions and challenge your thoughts.

Music is a tool you can use to help manage anxiety. What songs help you feel calm? When do you usually listen to these songs? What are the stories behind these songs? How can you incorporate music into your life to reduce anxiety?

_____

_____

_____

_____

_____

_____

_____

_____

_____

_____

_____

_____

_____

_____

_____

_____

_____

_____

reate a vision board and put it somewhere to remind you of your goals. Set a few goals and themes for your vision board. Find a piece of paper or cardboard and a few magazines. Cut out words and pictures that speak to you. Use words that describe how you want to feel. Use images of events you want to experience. This vision board is meant to be a representation of what you want out of life. Explore creative ways to lay out your pictures and words. Glue or tape the pictures and words onto the paper. If you are feeling extra inspired, add other arts and crafts to your board. How can you incorporate this vision board in your life to spark excitement? Find a spot to hang it in your house where you will pass by it and be reminded of the amazing things you want to accomplish.

Create a bucket list for the next five years. Write down 10 things you'd like to do. Describe your journeys in detail, such as trips you want to take, books you want to read, experiences you want to have, goals you want to achieve, and anything that will help create a more enriching life for yourself. If you completed your bucket list, how would your life look different? How can you overcome your anxiety to complete your list?

Anxiety can have benefits as well as drawbacks. One of the biggest benefits to anxiety is that it keeps us from engaging in dangerous activities, such as walking off cliffs, or shows us when someone is untrustworthy. How has having anxiety shaped you into the person you are today? Which of these aspects are you grateful for? How can you increase compassion for yourself around having anxiety?

My creative and positive energy is flowing through me all the time. I embrace creativity and positivity in my life.

Practice mindfulness with a body scan exercise and allow your body to relax. Find a comfortable space. Close your eyes. Begin scanning your body for any feelings of anxiety. Start with the top of your head. Notice any tenseness or other sensations you might be feeling. Allow the sensations to arise, without placing judgment on them as good or bad. Imagine white light coming into your body and releasing the tension. Once the tension is reduced, move on to the next part of your body, and gradually all the way down through your toes. Once you have scanned your whole body, bring your awareness back to the room. Open your eyes and notice how you feel as your body is in a relaxed state.

Write about someone who is significant in your life. How have they impacted you in a positive way? What would you like them to know about your relationship? How is this relationship impacted by your anxiety? Are there any changes you would like to make?

_____

_____

_____

_____

_____

_____

_____

_____

_____

_____

_____

_____

_____

_____

_____

_____

_____

Scheduling pleasurable activities is a fun and engaging way to decrease anxiety and increase joy. Pull out a weekly scheduler or calendar and mark off times in increments that work for you. One-hour increments are usually a good starting point. Fill in anything you must do, like work. Don't forget to include sleeping, eating, getting ready, commuting, and anything else that takes up time. Then look for times to insert fun activities. You can also schedule in time for self-care, meditation, exercise, and other healthy coping skills. Use the space provided to brainstorm fun activities and self-care. Create a schedule each week and set goals for your pleasurable pastimes. Look for areas in your life that are time wasters and begin to schedule healthy activities. How can you work on limiting activities that aren't supportive of your mental health? Reevaluate your values and incorporate activities based on what's important for you and your mental health.

Write about your favorite time of the year. Describe the rituals you have during that time. How is your anxiety impacted during your favorite time? How can you improve your overall mental health by celebrating your favorite time of the year?

_____

_____

_____

_____

_____

_____

_____

_____

_____

_____

_____

_____

_____

_____

_____

_____

_____

_____

My full potential will look different every day. I will try my best every day and be compassionate with myself.

Write a letter to your parents. Describe how you felt about them as a child. Tell them how you feel about them as an adult. Discuss how your feelings may have changed or stayed the same over the years. Share any unmet needs you may have now or in the past. Discuss your anxiety and your parents' role in it.

_____

_____

_____

_____

_____

_____

_____

_____

_____

_____

_____

_____

_____

_____

_____

_____

_____

_____

_____

Learn your triggers and create a plan for them. There are going to be things that trigger your anxiety, and you're not going to be able to control them. Examples of common anxiety triggers include health issues, financial concerns, negative thinking, social events, conflict, and relationship problems. You may do your best to avoid triggers, but you will not be able to avoid them all. You will need to come up with a plan to manage your triggers. Make a list of your triggers and then create a plan for each of them. For each trigger, write down two to three coping skills you can use when they occur. Use the exercises outlined in this journal as examples of healthy coping skills you can use. Put this plan somewhere that is easily accessible. Refer to this list often so you are prepared with your coping strategies. Review and revise them as needed and as you learn new ways to manage your anxiety.

S ometimes other emotions, such as sadness, anger, and shame, can feel overwhelming and worsen your anxiety. For example, if you feel sad about not being in a relationship, it can bring up a feeling of abandonment and trigger your anxiety. How do certain emotions impact your anxiety? What happens when you start to feel those emotions? What can you do to manage those emotions before they feel overwhelming?

Sleep is an important component of good physical and mental health. Anxiety can lead to trouble falling or staying asleep. It's helpful to learn strategies to turn off your brain at night. Try counting down from 100 by sevens until your body and mind relax. Sleep hygiene will help you sleep better: Try to use your bed only for sleeping. If you don't fall asleep within 15 to 20 minutes, get up and do something boring until you get sleepy again. Be patient with yourself when you have sleep problems, because beating yourself up or getting frustrated with the process may increase your anxiety. Stay away from electronics and bright lights for about an hour before you go to bed. Try picking up a book and reading a few pages to help you relax. The goal is to make your nighttime routine quiet and calming so your mind and body relax. When you are relaxed, you will be able to fall asleep quicker and stay asleep longer. Better-quality sleep leads to less anxiety and improved mental health.

Work on your relationship with your body image. Find a quiet place in your house. Light a candle and stand in front of a mirror. Begin slowly massaging your body. As you move through various parts of your body, recite a positive affirmation about your body. Keep the affirmation simple and something that is meaningful to you. If you notice any tension in any part of your body, put extra love and light into that area. The goal is to connect with your body in a positive way. If any negative thoughts come up, tell yourself that you are releasing any negative thoughts about your body that no longer serve you. As you finish with your massage, think about how you want to feel about yourself. Blow out your candle while setting the intention to feel that way whenever you can. Use this space to write out how you want to feel about yourself, as well as affirmations you can return to when you're feeling uncertain or negative about your body.

I am beautiful just the way I am.
I am wonderful just the way
I am. I accept who I am.

Write about how you give to others. Do you over-give or withdraw from other people? Write about how your patterns impact your relationships with others. Does your style of giving impact your anxiety? If so, what would you like to change?

Write a letter to someone who contributes to your anxiety. This letter can be to anyone in your environment, such as a friend, family member, or coworker, and in your life currently or from the past. Let them know how they contribute to your anxiety. Share with them how you would like their behavior to change. Even though you won't give them this letter, tell them what you would have liked from them, such as "I wish you would have supported my dreams."

Write about your job and career. How do they impact your anxiety? Describe the stressors of your job. What is the most stressful part of your work life? Which of these stressors do you have control over? Are there any changes you can make to reduce job stress?

_____

_____

_____

_____

_____

_____

_____

_____

_____

_____

_____

_____

_____

_____

_____

_____

_____

_____

Positive self-talk is a strategy you can use at any moment. Use the affirmations from this book as a starting point for your positive self-talk. Find sayings, quotes, and affirmations that are meaningful to you and repeat them. Use them when you are feeling anxious and when you feel calm. In moments of anxious feelings, stop and check in with your thoughts. Look for ways to change those thoughts into something positive. If you are thinking, *Nothing good ever happens to me*, change that thought to, *Good things happen to me when I least expect them*. Find ways to practice these positive thoughts at different times in your life. Create reminders throughout your day. Put positive statements in your phone as alarms that pop up. Write yourself sticky notes and leave them in random spots. Remind yourself to change your negative thinking to positive self-talk.

I can enjoy myself by relaxing and having fun. I will make time for activities I enjoy.

Being anxious in relationships is common, especially if you feel like you will be abandoned by your partner. How does your anxiety show up in relationships? Describe how you feel toward your romantic partner(s). What are you specifically anxious about in relationships, such as being abandoned, not having control, or thinking something bad will happen to your partner? How has anxiety created problems in your relationships? Does your anxiety relate to a fear of abandonment?

_____

_____

_____

_____

_____

_____

_____

_____

_____

_____

_____

_____

_____

_____

_____

_____

_____

Use problem-solving skills to reduce anxiety by putting yourself into action. There are some triggers that you can manage. The steps to problem-solving for anxiety include identifying the problem, creating a list of possible solutions, evaluating each solution, and picking the best outcome. It's important to push yourself outside of your comfort zone when problem-solving, especially where anxiety is concerned. This exercise will help you evaluate each of your solutions. Write down some solutions you have tried or want to try. For each solution, create a thorough pros and cons list. Some solutions that once seemed unrealistic may start to look achievable for you. Pick the best one based on the lists you've made. Once you implement your plan, reflect on how your option panned out and if you need to adjust your expectations, behaviors, or future planning.

I f someone you knew was struggling with anxiety, what would you tell them? How would you help them cope? Write down words of encouragement to help them get through their anxiety. Think about what you would want to hear and share those words.

_____

_____

_____

_____

_____

_____

_____

_____

_____

_____

_____

_____

_____

_____

_____

_____

_____

I am in charge of my life. Anxiety is not in charge of my life. I define my life in a way that brings joy.

On a scale of 1 to 10, with 1 being the least and 10 being the most, how peaceful are you today? Where would you say your day-to-day life fits on this scale? A three? A five? An eight? Can you recognize a range you most often find yourself in? How do you define peace in your life? What would be different if you felt more peaceful in your life? What can you do to increase tranquility in your life?

What are the three greatest lessons you have been taught about your anxiety? Write about each lesson and how it impacted you. Write a thank-you for each lesson to show gratitude. How can you increase gratitude in your life?

_____

_____

_____

_____

_____

_____

_____

_____

_____

_____

_____

_____

_____

_____

_____

_____

_____

Create a gratitude list when you start to feel down. Look for three to five experiences in your life you can be grateful for. Write them down to remind yourself to look for the good in your life. Then when you need them, you can list out things you are grateful for in your mind. Use this example as a guidepost: "I am thankful for (insert experience) because (insert reason why)." As you start to practice gratitude each day, you'll begin to see how your small experiences create a larger picture of good things you have in life. How can you incorporate gratitude when you feel anxious? How can expressing gratitude bring happiness to your life? Look for opportunities throughout your day to practice gratitude. Spend time in reflection each night and review your gratitude list. Make gratitude a part of the habits you create to decrease anxiety and increase happiness.

What are your three biggest strengths, such as your loving heart, wisdom, courage, determination, or patience? How do these strengths show up in your life? How can these strengths be used in the future to help manage anxiety?

se distraction tools to divert your attention from your anxiety. There are going to be moments when you cannot control your anxiety or reduce your triggers. A good way to manage your anxiety is to distract yourself. A common distraction tool you can use anywhere is to sing a song that repeats, like "Row, Row, Row Your Boat." Try singing the song in your mind if you can't sing it out loud. Repeat it several times until you begin to relax. If you can, sing aloud and allow the experience to turn into something fun and engaging. What are strategies you can use to begin to distract yourself when you feel anxious? Find small ways to distract your mind to reduce anxiety in stressful situations.

Make a list of 10 things that will bring a smile to your face. Think about small things like seeing a beautiful sunrise or big things like achieving a personal goal. Write about each of these things and how you can recognize them in your life on a regular basis. How has each of these things impacted your life and your anxiety?

_____

_____

_____

_____

_____

_____

_____

_____

_____

_____

_____

_____

_____

_____

_____

_____

_____

_____

_____

_____

Anxious thoughts and feelings leave me just as quickly as they come. I welcome loving and supportive thoughts.

Visualizing a safe, calm place can help you reduce anxiety. To create such a place, close your eyes and imagine a space where you feel safe and calm. What are the sights, sounds, and sensations connected to your space? What are you doing in your space? Is anyone else there? Think about how that place makes you feel. Focus on specific sensations and experiences to create a clear visualization of this space. Think of this place often, even before you begin to feel stressed or anxious. Whenever you do feel anxious, close your eyes and imagine your safe place. Recall the experience using your five senses. Once you are ready to leave your safe place, take a few deep breaths and then open your eyes. Find somewhere to put a picture of or an object from your safe place as a reminder of serenity.

What does it mean to you to be happy and fulfilled? What needs to be different in your life for you to be happy and fulfilled? How does anxiety impact your happiness? What obstacles are getting in the way of feeling fulfilled?

_____

_____

_____

_____

_____

_____

_____

_____

_____

_____

_____

_____

_____

_____

_____

_____

_____

Call upon your best self when you are feeling anxious. Your best self is the version of you that is happy, connected, thriving, and making the biggest impact in your world. When you start to feel agitated or overwhelmed, take a deep breath and ask yourself, "What would my best self do?" Repeat this question until you have an answer that makes sense for the situation. Another way to reframe this is to ask yourself, "How can I live my best life?" Continue to ask yourself these questions to help guide you through your daily life. Take some quiet time to reflect and visualize your best self and your best life. How would you respond to this trigger in that situation? What outcome would you like for yourself? What steps do you need to take in order to reach this peaceful outcome? Once you create a clear visualization, give yourself a pep talk about how you can and will achieve it. Tell a friend or a close confidant how you are planning to be your best self by engaging in behavior that aligns with how you really want to be. Write out some of your goals here, and list some examples of how you can redirect your thoughts when you are feeling anxious.

Imagine you are walking through nature. Describe your experience using all five senses: smell, sight, touch, sound, and taste. Where are you, and what do you see? How do you feel when you are in nature?

Seeing a messy work or living space can increase your anxiety and make you feel out of control. Look around your home, office, or anywhere else you spend lots of time. How do these spaces make you feel? What do you like and dislike about them? Think about what environment would make you feel calm and centered and what changes you can make in your space to achieve that goal. Throw out things that no longer bring you joy and look for ways to highlight the items that do bring you happiness. You could clean out your closet and donate clothes you haven't worn in a year or file your emails into folders. Look for ways you can organize your physical, virtual, and emotional spaces to feel more in control of your life. Create time in your schedule to regularly take stock of your surroundings and make the changes that make you feel safe.

How has journaling been going for you? What have you learned about yourself by journaling? How do you want your life to be different? How can you use what you learned to make lasting changes in your life?

_____

_____

_____

_____

_____

_____

_____

_____

_____

_____

_____

_____

_____

_____

_____

_____

_____

_____

After trying the techniques outlined in this book, which ones work best for you? Write yourself a self-care plan that outlines situations in which you can use your coping skills to calm down and stay centered. Review what works for you and what doesn't. Maybe you loved the body scan but a solo meditation is not helpful. Remember to "treat yourself" regularly. Create different plans for different situations: one plan for stressors at work, another plan for your triggers for anxiety, and yet another plan for how to manage relationship anxiety. Include five or more coping skills in your plan to use when you are experiencing a specific stressor. Having a plan can help reduce anxiety because you'll know that you can get control of your emotions. How can you use a self-care plan to make sure your needs are being met? Self-care is an important step to managing anxiety.

I accept responsibility for my anxiety. Although I cannot control how I feel, I can control how I respond to my feelings.

Conclusion

H ealing your anxiety and working through these practices, journaling questions, and affirmations is something to commend yourself on. It takes a lot of courage and perseverance to look inward and begin to explore the personal side of anxiety. Healing takes on many forms for women. You may find that journaling leads to a lot of self-discovery, which can be healing in and of itself. The more you know about yourself and why things happen the way they do, the more you become aware of how to best manage your behaviors and feelings; you cannot change what you are not aware of. For some women, the regular practice of good and healthy coping skills helps them create lasting change in their lives. For other women, affirmations serve as a constant reminder of their worth and their ability to manage anxiety even when they face adversity and challenges.

By working through this book, it's my hope for you that you find the one thing (or many things) that brings you hope, peace, and happiness. One part of working through this book is finding what works for you and brings you peace. You may find that you enjoy some activities more than others, and that's completely normal. Your anxiety may not go away completely. But by using this journal, you now have a guidepost for how to manage those feelings and symptoms when they start to emerge. Remind yourself that you are in control of your thoughts, feelings, and behaviors. Use the skills you learned to take back control of any part of your life that feels out of control.

By learning some strategies from cognitive behavioral therapy and dialectical behavioral therapy, you now have the foundation to move forward in your life with a plan for your anxiety. Use this journal often to reflect on your growth and change. The resources at the end of this book are for you to go deeper, if that is a part of your journey to managing your anxiety.

Resources

Big Magic by Elizabeth Gilbert
This book reminds us what to do when we face our deepest fears and need to do something big to work toward our dreams.

The Dialectical Behavior Therapy Skills Workbook for Anxiety by Alexander L. Chapman, PhD; Kim L. Gratz, PhD; and Matthew T. Tull, PhD
This workbook will teach you how to use dialectical behavioral therapy skills to manage your anxiety.

Feel the Fear and Do It Anyway by Susan Jeffers
The title tells you almost everything you need to know, but there are great strategies in this book to help you learn how to overcome your fears.

The Feeling Good Handbook by David D. Burns, MD
This book explains cognitive behavioral therapy and how to use it to manage anxiety.

The Gifts of Imperfection by Brené Brown
This book offers practical advice for women working on creating self-worth.

My Age of Anxiety by Scott Stossel
This memoir describes living with anxiety.

"Progressive Muscle Relaxation Script" by Therapist Aid. TherapistAid
.com/worksheets/progressive-muscle-relaxation-script.pdf
This script guides you through progressive muscle relaxations.

"Tips to Manage Anxiety and Stress" by the Anxiety & Depression Association of America (ADAA). ADAA.org/tips
This website offers resources for managing anxiety disorders.

"11 Tips for Coping with an Anxiety Disorder" by the Mayo Clinic Health System. MayoClinicHealthSystem.org/hometown-health /speaking-of-health/11-tips-for-coping-with-an-anxiety-disorder This list of coping tips includes links to additional resources from the Mayo Clinic.

References

"Any Anxiety Disorder." National Institute of Mental Health. Accessed December 5, 2021. NIMH.NIH.gov/health/statistics/any-anxiety -disorder.

Newman, Kira M. "How Journaling Can Help You in Hard Times." Greater Good Magazine. August 18, 2020. GreaterGood.Berkeley.edu /article/item/how_journaling_can_help_you_in_hard_times.

Ullrich, Philip M., and Susan K. Lutgendorf. "Journaling about Stressful Events: Effects of Cognitive Processing and Emotional Expression." *Annals of Behavioral Medicine* vol. 24, no. 3 (February 2002): 244–50. doi: 10.1207/S15324796ABM2403_10.

Acknowledgments

I have a loving and supportive husband, David, who told me, "Let's do this," when I shared about writing this book and the commitment it would take. Thank you for your continued support on our journey through life. Thank you to my sisters, Elizabeth, Kimberly, and Cathleen, who provided me with emotional support through my writings and my own anxieties. A special thank-you to the team at Caring Therapists, who inspire me to do big things for the mental health world. And finally, a big thank-you to my son, Ashton, who has shown me a new meaning of endless love.

About the Author

Amanda Landry is a licensed mental health counselor, certified addictions professional, and national certified counselor. She's the owner of the group practice Caring Therapists of Broward and Palm Beach in South Florida. Caring Therapists specializes in working with children through adults.

Amanda is trained in cognitive behavioral therapy (CBT), emotionally focused couples counseling, trauma-focused CBT, and eye movement desensitization and reprocessing (EMDR). Amanda specializes in treating anxiety and depression in teens and adults through holistic and evidence-based practices.

Amanda is the founder of My Private Practice Collective, an online community for therapists in private practice.

CPSIA information can be obtained
at www.ICGtesting.com
Printed in the USA
JSHW021745230222
23254JS00003B/6

9 781638 073611